Almost "Apple Hill" 1972–1980

It would be easy to say that Pathfinder School was the realization of a lifelong dream on the part of Arthur and Nancy Baxter, the fulfillment of an educational vision in-the-making over years of teaching.

But that wouldn't be exactly right. Pathfinder happened probably because it needed to happen, in the right time and in the right place, and because things came together at a certain moment. It was impelled by circumstances in one town and one family.

The Baxter family, six children, were happy enough in their decent county schools in Traverse City, Michigan. But it seemed to them and to their parents that there ought to be more. The spectacular beauty of the area with its pine-clad dunes, its deep blue bay dotted with sailboats, its snow-clad mornings of deep stillness— the availability of unusual experiences for families to take advantage of in one of the best out-of-doors in America, all called for some sort of unusual school experience too.

What could that be? Art and Nancy as teachers themselves were aware that much of public school teaching by necessity took place indoors, with schedules and routine curriculum guides. Routine schools had difficulty dealing with individuals. That was not to say that schools didn't try—and super teachers weren't testing the boundaries—they were. But the idea that a school could be quite different from the norm began to percolate in the Baxter family.

This group had its own experiences with private school education, which had the potential to be more individualized and interesting than schools which had to serve twenty-five or more students in a standard classroom. Art and Nancy had been at the Leelanau School, Art as headmaster and Nancy as AP and regular English teacher. Marybeth, then 13, was in her freshman year at Leelanau. John Baxter was at Interlochen, enrolled for cello study but excelling in academics. They all knew and respected the Independent School Association of the Central States, which set standards and aided private schools in Michigan.

of a school setting emerging from the mess, but the parents of 64 students were able to bridge that gap and the school opened with decent-sized classes in both lower and upper school.

A student who began the school as a sixth grader, and graduated from the Upper School (Class of '79), Jeff Lawson, recalls the first day of school in this new and hardly finished facility:

> I had had a bad year at Northport school and was ready to try anything, and I also found out the man who had been my teacher in the third grade at Northport, Alan Middleton, was going to be the sixth grade teacher. Got there the first day and our room was one of the ones still uncarpeted and almost no chairs. We sat around on the floor and discussed what we were going to do for the rest of the year. Two people were in the sixth grade. I was only 11 years old at that time, and I just wanted to get out of Northport school and saw Pathfinder as a good opportunity.

The state affirmed certification on the part of all teachers and the huge curriculum guide, actually a composite of several public and private plans for both Lower and Upper School, was accepted by the state of Michigan in August. Lower School teachers helped design that curriculum for their individual grades; Upper School teachers submitted plans for classes similar to the ones they had taught before, but with many more off-campus and innovative opportunities. Inspectors completed their inspections of the buildings and certified that they passed code. The junk pile was cleaned up out of the middle of the library, shelves were rolled across the room with broomsticks. and books (a few) appeared. Somebody donated a complete set of *National Geographic*s which looked appealing in their yellow covers on the library shelves, but which few students used.

A parent group organized itself. Early members were Maryann Force; Dr. and Mrs. Harry Blount; Mrs. and Mrs. Roger Watson; and Harry Oliver. They reviewed plans for the physical plant and curriculum along with the faculty. Dr. Blount became the first chairman of the board in the fall of 1972.

Reed became a fixture at the school and began his well-known and successful drama productions from Dr. Seuss, which toured schools in the Traverse area. He was named Director of Development.

The October, 1973 *Blazer* reported Mr. Zitting's impressions: "I like teaching, but the most important thing is that the students and I can share our thoughts and feelings about life." His drama programs were performed on makeshift stages, as shown on the next page.

Here are other Zitting comments, made in retrospect, about his experience at the school.

> Prior to Pathfinder I had been teaching theater at the Interlochen Arts Academy and was the Administrative Head of the Division of Art, Dance, and Drama. I resigned from the academy in protest to a new administration's edict containing many new rules defining student behavior and an attitude that didn't value faculty input in decision making. So I was a prime candidate to join Art and Nancy Baxter and the Pathfinder faculty. I had a healthy distrust of the bureaucratic process and that process was not in evidence at Pathfinder. I felt that education should be student-oriented rather than teacher-oriented and that decisions should be made with the students in mind first and then the faculty and then the administration. That was what was happening at Pathfinder. Art and Nancy felt that everyone should be in the classroom teaching, especially the head of the school, so that there would be no disconnect between decisions and the school family. It was like educational heaven to me, and I would say that to people when they asked me about the school.

Nancy Baxter says, "There is not enough good that can be said about Reed Zitting and his place as 'Second Founder' of the school. Reed became one of the foremost teacher-friends of students all over the campus. He was Art's and my best friend, co-planner of everything and always reliable help-mate. He directed the transition to new leadership eventually. In many ways, Reed Zitting represents the best of Pathfinder."

THE RADIO AUCTION AND
BEGINNINGS OF PATHFUNDER

One of the school's most enduring traditions, which would eventually be called PathFUNDer, began in 1977. Parents' Association members raised funds for scholarships at the "Radio Auction" in March. It offered services to bidders, kicking the effort off at a party at the Kellar of the Plantation Restaurant. Among the prizes up for bids were an airplane flight, a muzzle-loading rifle lesson, and a squirrel hunting expedition.

In the next few years the parent fund-raiser auctioned off a Lincoln Continental (1978), sponsored ever larger silent auctions, and raised tens of thousands of dollars of services and items for the scholarship fund.

Beyond that, however, was the friendship-building and loyalty-forging that went on through this process. Parents and administrators came to know each other closely, students pitched in with time and help, and the culminating evening was a huge public relations and get-to-know-Pathfinder success in the community. During these years the school also began its participation in the Cherry Festival parades, which extended its presence even further into the community. Teachers continued to consciously seek out interchange opportunities with the Traverse City public school community.

New teachers in the fall of '77 were Rich Hentschel teaching sixth grade and Mary Clark in the fifth grade room, with Judy Halsted enlarging and organizing the library. Sally Casey taught first graders. The Innisfree experience was bigger than ever, beginning September 21st with Grover Cleveland band rocking and rolling at night. The fall outing concluded with the usual giant pig roast. In November classes took vans to New Harmony in Indiana for environmental and history tours with Mr. Parks and "Mr. and Mrs. B."

Nineteen-seventy-seven rolled on past golden fall days into early snowfalls and cold winds of winter. Spelling bees, sock hops,

David Waltrip, a science teacher and educator, helped found Pathfinder.

Carlotta Schroeder was Pathfinder School's first graduate in 1973.

Humanities I class studied Cro-Magnon Man and cooked his typical foods. Tom Young, Lisa Hatlem, Mary Ann Bradford, Sharon Clancey, and John Baxter stir the fire.

Teacher Sue East shows Lower School students the bunnies as part of the early school's animals: chickens, ducks, peacocks, and the goat.

Al Brownlee helped plan the school and came from Appalachia with a music program.

Jerry Breu, "supe" of buildings and grounds, was a man for all seasons. He taught building skills, mowed the lawn, cooked soup, drove the van, and gave sage wisdom to teenagers who needed it.

The dock on Cedar Lake was packed at Potpourri time with those taking sailing—or ice-skating—lessons, depending on the season.

Betsy Nelson works with Becky Peasley.

Bayview Room
Mr. Johnson's class — (Standing Left to Right) — Susannah Gilmore, Robby Thompson, Mrs. Middleton, Mathew Ligon, Erik Scharf
Hicks, Mike Groleau, Mr. Johnson, (sitting) — Heather Smith, Tod Noordmans, Ed Rukowski, Scott Huggins, Steve Hall, Debbie Baumgar

Marty Trapp (not same as
above), French
Steve Weldon, music
Mary Lynn Watson, chemistry
Mary Zook, French

Jackie Bowen, financial
Ellen Northway, financial
Bob Prentice, maintenance
Mel Melzer, maintenance

Lower School

Patty Barrons
Sally Dunn
Pat Fulkerson
Mary Goeb
Peggy Heidel
Cindy Hogg
Jane Jason
Ted Johnson
Joyce MacManus
Greg North
Betsy Nelson
Patty Olson
Dick Parks
Robbi Rogers
Sharon Rutkowski
Steve Weldon

Staff

Chuck Gillies, Director I
Gabor Vazonyi, Director II
Reed Zitting. administrator
Bill Fortune, admissions
Bruce Matthews, admissions
Lynn James, secretary
Judy Weston, secretary

1986-1990 DR. MICHELLE JOHNSTON

In 1986 the school opened as a vibrant, forward-looking elementary school, pre-kindergarten through eighth grade. Dr. Michelle Johnston came to serve as Head of the School and remained in place—June 1986 through January 1990

Everyone (parents, teachers, Trustees, staff, and children) worked together with a renewed spirit of enthusiasm and cooperation to ready the campus for its new mission. There was also an air of excitement as the school began a new chapter in its history.

Joyce MacManus charts the life of the new Pathfinder elementary school:

> After two years Gabor moved on and we hired a new director. During Gabor's tenure we lost the high school. It was a low point in my time at Pathfinder. My son was going to be a senior when they closed the high school. I was afraid we might close the school altogether.
>
> Michelle Johnston was hired to direct a K-8 school. The space was more ample, but I missed the high school. Michelle was an excellent director having had experience in both Lower and Upper School. Michelle had two sons at Pathfinder, and that enhanced her commitment. We made some positive changes in curriculum during Michelle's years. Michelle left us to work on a program with Michigan State.

Dr. Michelle Johnston received her Ph.D. from Michigan State University in reading. She did postdoctoral work in psychology and taught school at the elementary level. Dr. Johnston spent part of her career as a reading consultant and had taught in the teacher education department at MSU as well as instructing in post-graduate courses to teachers through MSU Continuing Education Programs.

me, being the Director of Pathfinder School was an educational and professional development experience coupled with on-the-job training in financial management, thanks to Ellen Northway and many other supportive people, including Mike Dennos and Ward Haggard. Even Tom Lawton, retired treasurer of the Chrysler Corporation, helped me learn about budgets, projected revenues, expenses, and forecasting.

Every day, in my current position as a dean at a public university, I use those important skills that I learned at Pathfinder School more than I use many other concepts and understanding that I have learned in my graduate studies and through my life experiences. In fact, I also am an executive board member of a non-profit entity, and recently, I set up its budget structure which mirrors the Pathfinder structure. The other board members marveled at my financial expertise, an expertise that I learned during the summer of 1986.

However, that being said, the most important survival skill, which I learned during my Pathfinder tenure, was traffic direction. Every morning, noon, and afternoon, regardless of weather conditions, including freezing rain, icy sleet, or deep, wet lake-effect snow, I directed traffic at the bottom of the stairs. Because of the northern Michigan inclement weather, Tom bought me a rubberized raincoat, and Dee Haggard gave me a Donald Duck umbrella. I was grateful for the gifts because they were incredibly useful. As I opened car doors and directed parking, I met some very positive and talented children always eager to climb the stairs and go to class and their great parents whom I continue to see in the community. On occasions, I generated family-counseling hypotheses by observing seating arrangements in the cars.

Between 1986 and 1990, the library was the heart of the school as it was in the past. Generous donations of money and time by many Pathfinder friends, including Dee Haggard, ensured that the library remained a vibrant, integral underpinning of the school experience. In addition to housing its excellent collection, it was a place where students met for their town meetings, pizza lunches, stone semi-circle presentation, and celebrations of their heritage, learning, and

Sylvia Norris–music
Dick Parks–5-8 science
Lynn Pavlov–kindergarten
Sara Rodeck–art and art History
Robbi Rogers–fifth grade language arts and social studies
Sharon Rutkowski–French
Duncan Sprattmoran–6-8 grades language arts and social studies
Alice Waddington–fourth grade
Tracey Westerman–third grade
John Wunsch–fifth through eighth grade instrumental music

Staff:

Dr. Leonard Kupersmith–Headmaster
Ellen Northway–Business Manager
Bobbie Ames–assistant in business office
Terri Michael–School Secretary
Bobbie Stevens–Events and Information Coordinator and Summer Camp Director
Bob Prentice–Supervisor of Buildings and Grounds
Jim Hale–Maintenance
Marty Korwin-Pawlowski–Secretary

1991 Graduates
T. J. Hamilton
David Joynt

1992-1993 School Year

Faculty

Judy Bucciero–music
Susan Montgomery-Anderson–pre-kindergarten
Ray Fouch–5-8 grades Math
Pat Fulkerson–first grade
Mary Graves–aide, pre-kindergarten
Dawn Iott–lower elementary science, computers and logic
Joyce MacManus–second grade
Dick Parks–5-8 eighth grades science
Lynn Pavlov–kindergarten
Sara Rodeck–art and art history
Robbi Rogers–fifth grade language arts and social studies
Sharon Rutkowski–French
Susie Sawyer–physical education
Duncan Sprattmoran–6-8 grades language arts and social studies
Anita Summers–kindergarten
Alice Waddington–fourth grade
Tracey Westerman–third grade

On top of Notre Dame, March, 1990, (back) Matt Johnston, David Clark, Ben Maier, (front) Jana Detmer, Kendra Kearney.

Cloister at Mt. St. Michel, March, 1993. Molly Burder, Andrew Calcutt, Kaie Cilluffo, Theo Early, Christopher Kellog, Caitlin Smith, Kate Stilwill, Stephanie Swartzendruber, William Weiss, Sara Williams.

Mara Thompson
Leigh Ann Walters

2006-2007 Faculty

Paula Ward–preschool 3
Jorie Stryker–teacher's assistant
Andrea Hornby–pre-school 4
Jennifer Abel–kindergarten
Lynn Pavlov–first grade
T. Hanawalt–second grade
Joyce MacManus –third grade
Patty Barrons–fourth grade
Sally Gorenflo–fifth grade
Sarah Jane Johnson–sixth grade
language arts and social studies,
library
Duncan Sprattmoran–7/8 grades
language arts and social studies
Audrey Pittinos–5–8 Math
Dawn Iott–Lower School science
Shane Harrison–Middle School
science
Craig Fleuter–art
Karen McCarthy–French
Lynn Tobin–music
Kat Brown–dance
David Warne–percussion in-
structor
Susie Sawyer–phys. education
Merri Oberlin–technology
Susan Anderson-Hastings–
extended day

Staff

Mary Sue Wilkinson–Director
Ellen Northway–Associate Direc-
tor of Development
Barb Wilcox–Adm. Counselor
Robin Nance–Office Administra-
trator
Bob Prentice–Maintenance
Supervisor
Jim Hale–Custodian

2007 Graduates

Remington Barrett
Sam Cochran
Matthew Coobac
Benjamin Corwin
Justine Jaffe
Emily Kinney
Hannah Olson
Betsy Palisin
Aly Sarafa
Heather Skriba
Elizabeth Snodgrass
Jessica Thomas
Morgan Young

7th Grade 2001

Corey Adams

Rachel Cravit

Lindsay Hanson

Tyler Hsu

Katie Kass

Rachel Neithercut

Lillian Prentice

Cotopaxi Sprattmoran

Nora Stone

Kris Wietrick

Kelsey Wright

Not Pictured:
Amy Woodward

Kelsey and Nora

Rachel

Lily, Kristen, Katie, Rachel and Lindsay

Mrs. Merrill

Oliver Box

Lauren Bruno

Miles Carey

Logan Dell'Acqua

Christina Fragel

Brianne Munch

Skyler Norgaard

Abigail Palisin

Rory Womack

Helen Montie

Mrs. Merrill - Fourth Grade

The smell of Rotten Eggs and the Sight of Snow on the Branches
John Baxter, Class of 1974
Account Executive, SAP Corporation

For me, Pathfinder offered an ideal combination of small classes and inspired teaching. One example was my Chemistry course with Mrs. Watson. Matt Sullivan and I had the privilege of being the two students to inaugurate Pathfinder's chem lab, and Mrs. Watson was our guide. She had an amazing ability to explain difficult mathematical concepts in understandable ways; and then to show us how that math came to life in the lab. We created aromatic concoctions, induced flames to burst from glassware, and produced the most wonderfully colored liquids that would turn from hot to cold...all predicted through math and confirmed through observation. It was a marvelous introduction to the physical sciences, and inspired me to pursue a career that combined math and science...engineering.

Another example of inspired teaching in small classes was my mother's English classes. Held in the art annex, in a room not far from the pottery wheels, the six seniors would sit in comfortable bean bag chairs and consider Shakespeare and other English masters. As snowflakes fell gently outside and created a winter wonderland in the pines and hardwoods outside our window, we would read, debate, and consider the meaning and lessons from the great works in English. My mother had a natural way with seventeen-year-olds, and was a master of her subject. From her, we learned the fundamentals of critical thinking and clear communication, which provided a foundation for our college and professional success.

Pathfinder enabled a diverse group of kids to experience learning in a fresh, innovative way, and with its outstanding faculty dedicated to inspired teaching I gained an invaluable foundation that served me well in college and life.